JOSHUA LEE BRYANT

The Psychology of Selling: Mastering the Art of Influence

Joshua Lee Bryant

First published by Joshua Lee Bryant 2023

Copyright © 2023 by Joshua Lee Bryant

All rights reserved. No part of this publication may be reproduced, stored or transmitted in any form or by any means, electronic, mechanical, photocopying, recording, scanning, or otherwise without written permission from the publisher. It is illegal to copy this book, post it to a website, or distribute it by any other means without permission.

Joshua Lee Bryant asserts the moral right to be identified as the author of this work.

Designations used by companies to distinguish their products are often claimed as trademarks. All brand names and product names used in this book and on its cover are trade names, service marks, trademarks and registered trademarks of their respective owners. The publishers and the book are not associated with any product or vendor mentioned in this book. None of the companies referenced within the book have endorsed the book.

First edition

*This book was professionally typeset on Reedsy.
Find out more at reedsy.com*

Contents

Preface		v
Acknowledgement		vii
1	Chapter 1: The Fundamentals of Psychology in Sales	1
	1.1 The Human Mind: Understanding Your Customer	3
	1.2 Cognitive Biases: Exploiting the Mind's Shortcuts	7
	1.3 Emotional Intelligence: Connecting with Your Prospects	11
2	Chapter 2: Building Trust and Rapport	16
	2.1 The Power of First Impressions	19
	2.2 Active Listening: The Key to Connection	23
	2.3 Mirroring and Matching: The Art of Subtle Influence	26
3	Chapter 3: Persuasion Techniques	29
	3.1 The Six Principles of Persuasion	30
	3.2 Storytelling: Captivate Your Audience	34
	3.3 Framing: The Art of Contextualizing Your Message	38
4	Chapter 4: Overcoming Objections and Resistance	42
	4.1 Identifying and Classifying Objections	42
	4.2 Dealing with Resistance: Turning 'No' into 'Yes'	44
5	Chapter 5: Closing the Deal	50
6	Chapter 6: The Salesperson's Mindset	57

6.1 Building Resilience: Overcoming Rejection and Failure	60
6.2 Goal Setting and Motivation	62
6.3 Continuous Learning and Self-Improvement	65
7 Chapter 7: Advanced Sales Techniques	69
8 Chapter 8: Digital Sales and the Future of Selling	75
8.1 The Power of Social Media and Content Marketing	78
8.2 Email Marketing: Crafting Compelling Sales Messages	81
8.3 The Role of Artificial Intelligence in Sales	84
9 Chapter 9: Building A Successful Marketing Campaign	87
9.1 Different Types Of Ads	91
9.2 Ad Strategies	94
10 Chapter 10: Conclusion	99
About the Author	103

Preface

In today's competitive and rapidly evolving marketplace, the ability to sell effectively has never been more crucial. Whether you are a seasoned sales professional or just starting in the field, understanding the psychological underpinnings of the sales process can provide you with a significant advantage. It is with this in mind that I have written "The Psychology of Selling: Mastering the Art of Influence," a comprehensive guide to the myriad psychological factors that drive the sales process, and practical strategies for leveraging these insights to achieve success in the world of selling.

As a marketing consultant, I have come to realize that the most important aspect of a successful marketing campaign is a solid sales strategy that builds off of advertisement efforts. In my years of experience, I have observed countless sales professionals and entrepreneurs struggle to convert leads into customers, despite having a stellar marketing campaign. This observation led me to explore the art of selling more deeply, delving into the psychological factors that contribute to successful sales interactions.

In this book, you will find a wealth of information on topics ranging from the fundamentals of psychology in sales to the intricate art of persuasion. We will discuss the importance of building trust and rapport, the power of storytelling, and the role of emotional intelligence in connecting with your prospects. Furthermore, we will explore the impact of technology on sales, including the rise of digital sales channels, social media, and artificial intelligence.

Throughout the chapters, I have sought to strike a balance between theory and practice, providing not only an understanding of the psychological principles at play but also offering actionable strategies and techniques that can be applied immediately to improve your sales performance. My hope is that this book will serve as a valuable resource for anyone seeking to hone their sales skills, deepen their understanding of the psychology of selling, and ultimately, master the art of influence.

As you embark on this journey to uncover the secrets of the psychology of selling, I encourage you to approach the material with an open mind and a willingness to learn. By doing so, you will be better equipped to adapt your sales approach to the unique needs and desires of your prospects, and in turn, achieve greater success in the world of selling.

Welcome to "The Psychology of Selling: Mastering the Art of Influence." May you find the insights and strategies contained within these pages to be transformative in your journey toward sales excellence.

Acknowledgement

Writing "The Psychology of Selling: Mastering the Art of Influence" has been a labor of love, and I am deeply grateful for the support and encouragement I have received from numerous individuals along the way.

First and foremost, I would like to express my profound gratitude to my loving partner, Carrissa. Your unwavering support, understanding, and patience throughout this journey have been invaluable. I am eternally grateful for your presence in my life, and your love has been a constant source of strength and inspiration. As we anticipate the arrival of our baby later this year, I look forward to the new adventures that lie ahead for our growing family.

I would also like to extend my heartfelt thanks to my mentors and colleagues who have generously shared their wisdom, experience, and insights with me. Your guidance and encouragement have played an essential role in the development of this book.

Finally, I would like to thank you, the reader, for embarking on this journey with me. I hope that you find the insights and strategies within these pages to be both transformative and empowering as you strive to achieve success in the world of selling.

Thank you all for your contributions, support, and for being a part of this incredible journey.

1

Chapter 1: The Fundamentals of Psychology in Sales

In the world of sales, understanding the psychological principles that influence human behavior can provide a significant advantage. By leveraging the fundamentals of psychology, sales professionals can better connect with their prospects, build trust, and ultimately close more deals. In this chapter, we will explore the key psychological concepts that underpin successful selling and provide a solid foundation for mastering the art of influence.

The Role of Emotions in Decision-Making

Emotions play a crucial role in the decision-making process. While people often believe that their choices are driven by rational thought, research has shown that emotions frequently guide decision-making. In the context of sales, understanding the emotional needs of your prospects and appealing to their emotions can significantly influence their buying decisions.

For example, creating a sense of urgency or scarcity can trigger the fear of missing out (FOMO) in prospects, making them more likely to commit to a purchase. Similarly, presenting your product or service as a solution to a problem can evoke a sense of relief and satisfaction, increasing the likelihood of a sale.

Building Trust and Rapport

Trust and rapport are essential components of any successful sales relationship. When prospects trust a sales professional, they are more likely to open up about their needs, listen to recommendations, and ultimately, make a purchase.

Establishing trust and rapport begins with understanding your prospect's needs and demonstrating genuine empathy. This can be achieved by actively listening to your prospects, asking open-ended questions, and validating their concerns. By showing that you truly understand and care about their needs, you can create a strong foundation for a successful sales relationship.

Social Proof and the Power of Consensus

Social proof is a powerful psychological principle that can be leveraged to influence prospects in the sales process. People are more likely to trust and follow the actions of others, especially when they are uncertain about what to do. By providing evidence of other customers who have had success with your product or service, you can tap into this powerful psychological driver to persuade your prospects.

AN UPPERCASE CREATIVE PROMPT

Fleeting thoughts...

Our thought process can be more interesting than polished results. Document your ideas as they change shape.

AN UPPERCASE CREATIVE PROMPT

Growth.

Is your growth as a creative person branching up and spreading out or is it found in rooting more deeply?

AN UPPERCASE CREATIVE PROMPT

Creative time.

What is the smallest amount of time that you need in order to be creative? A second? A few minutes? A lifetime?

AN UPPERCASE CREATIVE PROMPT

revisit, review, remix, revise

Revisit your older work.

How can you remix or revise it to represent who you are in the present moment?

AN UPPERCASE CREATIVE PROMPT

Find your landscape.

What natural landscape would you pick to express your creative personality? What are the textures and palettes of these natural places?

U

AN UPPERCASE CREATIVE PROMPT

How can you bring depth to your work?

Through emotion, research, technique— or perhaps all three?

U

AN UPPERCASE CREATIVE PROMPT

Quiet time.

Creativity requires periods of silence.

U

AN UPPERCASE CREATIVE PROMPT

To make art, you need two driving forces: inspiration and impulse.

U

Examples of social proof in sales include sharing customer testimonials, case studies, and industry awards. By showcasing the success of others, you can help alleviate any doubts or concerns your prospects may have, making them more likely to commit to a purchase.

The Principle of Reciprocity

The principle of reciprocity is another fundamental aspect of human psychology that can be harnessed in the sales process. People have a natural tendency to want to repay favors or acts of kindness, creating a sense of obligation that can be leveraged to influence decision-making.

In sales, reciprocity can be employed by offering something of value to your prospects, such as a free consultation, trial, or valuable content. By providing value upfront, you can create a sense of indebtedness in your prospects, making them more likely to reciprocate by engaging in a sales conversation or making a purchase.

1.1 The Human Mind: Understanding Your Customer

As a sales professional, your success largely depends on your ability to understand your customers and connect with them on a deeper level. To do this, you must first gain insight into the human mind and learn how it processes information, makes decisions, and interacts with the world around it. In this section, we will explore the psychology behind human behavior, decision-making, and social interactions, all of which will help you build stronger connections with your prospects and close more deals.

The Decision-Making Process

Understanding how people make decisions is crucial in the sales process, as it will allow you to adapt your sales techniques to better align with your prospect's thought process. The human mind relies on two primary systems when making decisions:

1. **System 1:** This is our intuitive and automatic thinking system. It is fast, emotional, and based on instincts and personal experiences. System 1 is responsible for making quick decisions, such as reacting to a potential threat or recognizing familiar faces.
2. **System 2:** This is our slow, analytical thinking system. It is responsible for processing complex information, problem-solving, and making deliberate decisions. System 2 requires more cognitive effort and is engaged when we weigh the pros and cons of a decision or solve a mathematical problem.

In sales, it is essential to recognize when your prospect is using System 1 or System 2 thinking and adjust your approach accordingly. For example, when presenting the benefits of your product or service, you can appeal to System 1 by evoking emotions and telling relatable stories, while also providing data and logical arguments to engage System 2.

CHAPTER 1: THE FUNDAMENTALS OF PSYCHOLOGY IN SALES

Emotions in Decision-Making

Emotions play a significant role in the decision-making process. Studies have shown that people often rely on their emotions when making decisions, especially when they feel overwhelmed by information or are under time constraints. As a salesperson, you can leverage this knowledge by appealing to your prospect's emotions, making them more likely to choose your product or service.

Some ways to evoke emotions in your sales pitch include:

1. **Creating a sense of urgency:** People are more likely to act when they feel that they may miss out on an opportunity. Use time-sensitive offers or highlight limited availability to create a sense of urgency.
2. **Using storytelling:** Share success stories and testimonials from satisfied customers to evoke emotions such as trust, happiness, and security.
3. **Identifying pain points:** Understand your prospect's pain points and demonstrate how your product or service can alleviate their problems, evoking emotions of relief and hope.

Social Influence

People are heavily influenced by the opinions and actions of others, a concept known as social influence. This can be seen in various psychological phenomena, such as conformity, social proof, and authority. In sales, you can use these principles to your advantage:

1. **Conformity:** People are more likely to make a purchase if they believe that others are doing the same. Showcase the popularity of your product or service by sharing statistics, social media engagement, or testimonials.
2. **Social proof:** Prospects are more likely to trust your product or service if they see that others have had positive experiences with it. Provide reviews, case studies, and endorsements to build credibility and trust.
3. **Authority:** People are more likely to trust and follow the advice of experts or authoritative figures. Establish yourself as an expert in your field by sharing your knowledge, experience, and credentials.

By understanding the human mind and how it processes information, makes decisions, and interacts with others, you can tailor your sales approach to better connect with your prospects and influence their decisions.

Case Study: The Power of Social Proof in Sales (Cialdini et al., 1975)

One of the most well-known studies on the psychology of sales was conducted by Robert Cialdini and his colleagues in 1975. The researchers aimed to understand the impact of social proof on consumer behavior by manipulating the number of people who were observed engaging in a specific action. In their experiment, they had a confederate stare up at the sky in a busy public area. When only one person was looking up, 42% of passers-by also looked up. However, when a group of five confederates stared up at the sky, 83% of passers-by followed suit.

This study demonstrated the power of social proof in influencing decision-making, and its findings have significant implications for sales professionals. By highlighting the popularity of a product or service and showcasing testimonials or endorsements, salespeople can capitalize on the natural human tendency to follow the actions of others.

Reference: Cialdini, R. B., Levy, A., Herman, C. P., Kozlowski, L. T., & Petty, R. E. (1975). Elastic Shift of Opinion: Determinants of Direction and Durability. Journal of Personality and Social Psychology, 32(2), 260-270.

1.2 Cognitive Biases: Exploiting the Mind's Shortcuts

Cognitive biases are systematic errors in thinking that affect the decisions and judgments people make. These biases often result from the brain's attempt to simplify information processing, leading to shortcuts that can be both helpful and harmful. As a salesperson, understanding these cognitive biases can help you create more persuasive sales pitches and navigate potential obstacles in the sales process.

In this chapter, we will explore some of the most common cognitive biases and how you can exploit them in your sales efforts.

The Anchoring Bias

The anchoring bias occurs when people rely too heavily on an initial piece of information (the "anchor") to make subsequent decisions. This can significantly impact their perception of value and willingness to spend money.

In sales, you can use the anchoring bias to your advantage by setting a high initial price or comparing your product to a more expensive competitor. This will make your offering seem more valuable and affordable in comparison, increasing the likelihood of a sale.

The Confirmation Bias

The confirmation bias refers to the tendency to favor information that confirms one's existing beliefs or values, while disregarding information that contradicts them. This can result in selective attention and interpretation of information, leading to flawed decision-making.

To exploit the confirmation bias in sales, focus on presenting information that aligns with your prospect's existing beliefs or preferences. This will make them more receptive to your message and more likely to accept your offering. Additionally, be prepared to address any objections or concerns by providing evidence that supports your claims, without directly contradicting their beliefs.

The Availability Heuristic

The availability heuristic is a mental shortcut that leads people to judge the likelihood of an event based on the ease with which relevant examples come to mind. This can result in an overestimation of the probability of certain outcomes, based on the vividness or recency of the examples.

In sales, you can leverage the availability heuristic by sharing vivid, memorable stories about satisfied customers or the success of your product. This will make your offering seem more desirable and effective, increasing the likelihood of a sale.

The Loss Aversion Bias

Loss aversion is the tendency for people to prefer avoiding losses rather than acquiring equivalent gains. In other words, the pain of losing is psychologically more powerful than the pleasure of gaining.

To capitalize on loss aversion in your sales approach, emphasize the potential losses your prospect might face if they don't purchase your product or service. This could include missed opportunities, financial losses, or negative consequences related to their problem. By focusing on the potential losses, you can increase the perceived value of your offering and motivate prospects to take action.

The Reciprocity Principle

The reciprocity principle states that people feel an inherent obligation to repay favors or gifts, even if they are unsolicited. This can create a strong psychological urge to reciprocate, influencing people's behavior and decision-making.

In the context of sales, you can use the reciprocity principle by offering something of value to your prospect, such as free samples, valuable content, or personalized advice. This will make them more likely to feel indebted to you and more inclined to do business with you in return.

By understanding and exploiting these cognitive biases, you can create more persuasive sales pitches and effectively influence your prospects' decision-making process. Keep in mind that using these biases ethically and responsibly is critical; manipulation or deceitful practices can harm your reputation and negatively impact your long-term success.

1.3 Emotional Intelligence: Connecting with Your Prospects

Emotional intelligence (EI) is the ability to recognize, understand, and manage both your own emotions and the emotions of others. In sales, developing a high level of emotional intelligence is essential for building strong connections with your prospects, navigating difficult conversations, and ultimately closing deals. This section will explore the key components of emotional intelligence and provide practical strategies for enhancing your EI in the sales process.

The Four Components of Emotional Intelligence

Emotional intelligence consists of four primary components:

- **Self-awareness:** The ability to recognize and understand your own emotions, as well as their impact on your thoughts, behaviors, and interactions with others.
- **Self-management:** The ability to regulate your emotions and respond to situations in an appropriate and constructive manner.
- **Social awareness:** The ability to recognize and understand the emotions and perspectives of others, including their needs, motivations, and concerns.
- **Relationship management:** The ability to build and maintain healthy relationships with others by effectively communicating, empathizing, and resolving conflicts.

Developing Self-Awareness in Sales

In sales, self-awareness is crucial for recognizing your own emotional triggers and biases, understanding how they may affect your interactions with prospects, and making adjustments to improve your communication and rapport-building skills. To enhance your self-awareness, consider the following strategies:

1. **Reflect on your emotions:** Regularly take time to assess your emotional state and identify any emotions that may be influencing your thoughts and behaviors.
2. **Seek feedback:** Ask colleagues, mentors, or trusted friends for feedback on your communication and interpersonal skills. This can help you identify areas for improvement and gain new insights into your emotional patterns.
3. **Keep a journal:** Documenting your emotions, thoughts, and experiences can help you gain a deeper understanding of your emotional triggers and patterns, as well as their impact on your sales interactions.

Mastering Self-Management in Sales

Effective self-management is essential for maintaining a positive and professional demeanor in the face of challenges, objections, or setbacks during the sales process. To improve your self-management skills, consider the following tips:

1. **Develop healthy coping mechanisms:** Practice stress-reduction techniques, such as deep breathing exercises, mindfulness meditation, or physical activity, to help you

manage negative emotions and maintain a calm, focused mindset.
2. **Set realistic goals:** Establish clear, attainable goals for your sales performance and track your progress. This can help you maintain motivation and manage feelings of frustration or disappointment.
3. **Cultivate a growth mindset:** Embrace challenges and setbacks as opportunities for learning and growth, rather than viewing them as indicators of failure.

Enhancing Social Awareness in Sales

Social awareness is critical for understanding your prospects' emotions, needs, and motivations, allowing you to better tailor your sales approach and create a more personalized, impactful experience. To develop your social awareness, consider the following strategies:

- **Practice active listening:** Focus on truly understanding your prospect's concerns, needs, and desires by asking open-ended questions, paraphrasing their statements, and providing verbal and non-verbal cues to demonstrate your attentiveness.
- **Develop empathy:** Put yourself in your prospect's shoes and try to understand their perspective, emotions, and motivations. This will help you build rapport and establish trust.
- **Observe non-verbal cues:** Pay attention to body language, facial expressions, and tone of voice to gain insights into your prospect's emotional state and level of interest.

Strengthening Relationship Management in Sales

Effective relationship management is essential for building lasting connections with your prospects and ensuring long-term sales success. To enhance your relationship management skills, always remember that the goal is not only to complete the sale but develop a "friend-like" relationship with the client so they will know that they can count on you to be there for them. This will increase the LTV (lifetime value) of the client.

While remaining professional, you always can go above & beyond to satisfy the potential customer's desire to be understood, heard, and made to feel like their best interest is considered with your intentions.

> **Case Study: The Role of Reciprocity in Sales**
>
> *In a study by Regan (1971), participants were asked to rate various pieces of art. During the experiment, a confederate either gave the participant a soft drink as a gift or did not give them a gift. Afterward, the confederate asked the participant to buy raffle tickets. The results showed that participants who received the soft drink were more likely to buy raffle tickets and, on average, purchased more tickets than those who did not receive a gift.*
>
> *This study demonstrates the power of the principle of reciprocity in sales. When sales professionals provide value or offer something of value to prospects, those prospects are more likely to feel compelled to reciprocate, increasing the likelihood of making a purchase.*

Reference: Regan, D. T. (1971). Effects of a favor and liking on compliance. Journal of Experimental Social Psychology, 7(6), 627–639.

2

Chapter 2: Building Trust and Rapport

In the world of sales, building trust and rapport with your prospects is essential for successful outcomes. When prospects feel a connection with a sales professional and trust their intentions, they are more likely to share their needs, concerns, and desires. This openness allows for a more effective sales conversation, which can ultimately lead to a successful deal. In this chapter, we will explore the key elements and strategies for building trust and rapport with your prospects, ensuring you create strong foundations for a successful sales relationship.

Understanding Your Prospects

The first step in building trust and rapport is to truly understand your prospects. This involves getting to know their needs, desires, and pain points. By understanding what motivates them and what challenges they face, you can tailor your sales approach to address their specific concerns and demonstrate genuine empathy.

To gain a deeper understanding of your prospects, consider conducting thorough research on their industry, company, and role. This will enable you to ask informed questions and engage in meaningful conversations that show your genuine interest in their situation.

Active Listening

Active listening is a crucial skill for establishing trust and rapport with your prospects. By truly hearing and understanding what they are saying, you can demonstrate empathy and convey that their needs and concerns are important to you.

To practice active listening, make a conscious effort to fully focus on your prospect's words and avoid interrupting them. Give them the space to express themselves, and resist the urge to formulate your response while they are speaking. Instead, take a moment to process their thoughts and ask follow-up questions to clarify and demonstrate your understanding.

Open and Honest Communication

Open and honest communication is essential for building trust and rapport in any relationship, including sales interactions. By being transparent and sincere with your prospects, you can establish a sense of credibility and reliability, which are essential for fostering trust.

To facilitate open and honest communication, be upfront about your intentions and avoid using high-pressure sales tactics. Focus on creating a genuine connection with your prospect, sharing your expertise and insights to help them make an informed decision.

Consistency and Reliability

Consistency and reliability play a significant role in building trust and rapport with your prospects. By consistently following through on your commitments and delivering on your promises, you demonstrate that you are a trustworthy and dependable partner.

To establish consistency and reliability, ensure that you meet deadlines, keep appointments, and deliver on any promises you make. If you encounter any obstacles or delays, communicate proactively with your prospects, providing updates and alternative solutions to maintain their trust.

Finding Common Ground

Finding common ground with your prospects can help establish rapport and create a sense of connection. By identifying shared interests, values, or experiences, you can build a foundation for a strong relationship.

To find common ground with your prospects, listen actively for any shared experiences or interests during your conversations. When you identify a connection, engage in a genuine conversation about the topic, demonstrating your enthusiasm and creating a sense of camaraderie.

CHAPTER 2: BUILDING TRUST AND RAPPORT

2.1 The Power of First Impressions

First impressions play a crucial role in the sales process, as they can significantly influence a prospect's perception of you and your product or service. Research shows that people form initial impressions within seconds of meeting someone, and these impressions can be difficult to change. Therefore, it is essential to make a positive and lasting first impression to increase your chances of sales success. In this section, we will explore the factors that contribute to first impressions and provide strategies for making a strong and memorable impact on your prospects.

Factors Influencing First Impressions

Several factors contribute to the formation of first impressions, including:

- **Appearance:** Your physical appearance, including clothing, grooming, and body language, can significantly impact how others perceive you. Dressing professionally and maintaining a clean, polished appearance can help establish credibility and trust with your prospects.
- **Communication style:** Your tone of voice, choice of words, and clarity in communication can shape your prospect's perception of your competence and confidence. Speak clearly, confidently, and use language that is appropriate for your audience.
- **Attitude:** Your attitude, including your level of enthusiasm,

positivity, and openness, can influence how others perceive you. A positive, friendly attitude can help create rapport and make prospects more receptive to your message.

Strategies for Making a Positive First Impression

To make a strong and lasting first impression on your prospects, consider the following strategies:

1. **Be punctual:** Arriving on time for meetings or calls demonstrates respect for your prospect's time and shows that you are organized and reliable.
2. **Smile and make eye contact:** A genuine smile and maintaining eye contact during your initial interaction can create a sense of warmth and trust, making your prospect feel more at ease.
3. **Practice active listening:** Show your prospect that you value their thoughts and opinions by engaging in active listening, which involves maintaining eye contact, nodding, and asking open-ended questions to encourage further conversation.
4. **Demonstrate confidence:** Stand tall, maintain a firm handshake, and speak confidently and clearly to project an image of competence and credibility.
5. **Be authentic:** Be genuine and true to your personality, values, and beliefs. People are more likely to trust and connect with someone who is authentic and sincere.
6. **Be prepared:** Research your prospect and their needs before your initial interaction. This will help you tailor your pitch to their specific interests and demonstrate your

knowledge and expertise.

Overcoming a Negative First Impression

If you believe you have made a negative first impression, it is essential to address the issue promptly and attempt to repair the relationship. Consider the following strategies to overcome a negative first impression:

1. **Acknowledge the issue:** If you are aware of a specific mistake or miscommunication that led to the negative impression, address it openly and apologize if necessary.
2. **Demonstrate consistency:** Show your prospect that the negative impression was an isolated incident by consistently demonstrating professionalism, competence, and reliability in your subsequent interactions.
3. **Build rapport:** Make an effort to connect with your prospect on a personal level by engaging in small talk, showing empathy, and finding common interests.
4. **Provide value:** Demonstrate your expertise and commitment to your prospect's success by offering valuable insights, resources, or solutions to their problems.

By understanding the factors that contribute to first impressions and implementing strategies to make a positive and lasting impact on your prospects, you can significantly improve your chances of sales success and establish strong, trusting relationships with your clients.

Case Study: The Impact of Priming on Sales

In a study conducted by Naomi Mandel and Eric J. Johnson, researchers explored the impact of priming on consumer behavior. They set up an online store and manipulated the background design to include either a green or a red background. Customers who viewed the store with a green background were primed with the concept of money, while those who viewed the store with a red background were not. The results showed that customers exposed to the green background spent significantly less than those exposed to the red background (Mandel & Johnson, 2002).

This study highlights the importance of understanding how subtle cues in the sales environment can prime prospects to behave in specific ways. By being aware of the psychological impact of various elements in the sales process, sales professionals can optimize their approach to create a more conducive environment for closing deals.

Reference: Mandel, N., & Johnson, E. J. (2002). When web pages influence choice: Effects of visual primes on experts and novices. Journal of Consumer Research, 29(2), 235-245.

2.2 Active Listening: The Key to Connection

Active listening is a vital skill for sales professionals, as it allows you to truly understand your prospect's needs, concerns, and motivations. By engaging in active listening, you can build trust, rapport, and connection with your prospects, making them more receptive to your message and ultimately increasing your chances of closing a deal. In this section, we will explore the principles of active listening and provide practical tips for enhancing your listening skills in the sales process.

The Principles of Active Listening

Active listening involves fully focusing, understanding, and responding to your prospect's words, emotions, and body language. It goes beyond merely hearing what is being said and requires a conscious effort to engage in the conversation. The key principles of active listening include:

- **Giving your full attention:** Focus solely on your prospect and their message, avoiding distractions and the temptation to mentally prepare your response while they are still speaking.
- **Non-verbal communication:** Pay attention to your prospect's body language, facial expressions, and tone of voice, as these can provide valuable insights into their emotions and state of mind.
- **Reflecting and paraphrasing:** Summarize your prospect's message in your own words to demonstrate your under-

standing and encourage further conversation.
- **Asking open-ended questions:** Use open-ended questions to encourage your prospect to elaborate on their thoughts, feelings, and concerns, providing you with valuable information to tailor your sales pitch.
- **Providing feedback:** Offer verbal and non-verbal cues, such as nodding, smiling, or saying "I understand," to show that you are engaged and attentive.

Enhancing Your Active Listening Skills in Sales

To improve your active listening skills in the sales process, consider the following strategies:

1. **Minimize distractions:** Eliminate any distractions, such as background noise, electronic devices, or interruptions, to ensure you can fully focus on your prospect.
2. **Practice patience:** Allow your prospect to finish speaking before responding or asking questions, even if there is a pause or silence in the conversation. This demonstrates respect for their thoughts and opinions.
3. **Cultivate empathy:** Put yourself in your prospect's shoes and try to understand their emotions, concerns, and motivations. This will help you connect on a deeper level and create a sense of trust and rapport.
4. **Avoid interrupting:** Refrain from interrupting your prospect, even if you disagree with their statement or have an important point to make. Instead, wait for an appropriate moment to express your thoughts or ask questions.

5. **Take notes:** Jot down key points and important information during your conversation, as this will help you remember and reflect on your prospect's needs and concerns later in the sales process.

The Benefits of Active Listening in Sales

Developing strong active listening skills can provide numerous benefits in the sales process, including:

- **Building trust and rapport:** By demonstrating genuine interest and understanding of your prospect's needs and concerns, you can establish a strong foundation of trust and rapport, making them more likely to engage with you and consider your offering.
- **Gathering valuable information:** Active listening allows you to collect crucial information about your prospect's needs, preferences, and pain points, enabling you to tailor your sales approach and address their specific concerns effectively.
- **Reducing misunderstandings:** By engaging in active listening, you can minimize the likelihood of miscommunication or misunderstandings, ensuring that both you and your prospect are on the same page.
- **Enhancing problem-solving:** Active listening helps you identify the root causes of your prospect's concerns or objections, allowing you to present targeted solutions that address their needs directly.

By mastering the principles of active listening and incorporating these strategies into your sales approach, you not only increase your chances of closing the deal with your prospective customer but you leave a good impression on them. I would personally consider a conversation with a salesman/woman a positive one if I knew that they actually were listening to me during our conversation.

2.3 Mirroring and Matching: The Art of Subtle Influence

Mirroring and matching are powerful psychological techniques used to establish rapport and create a sense of connection with your prospects. By subtly mimicking your prospect's body language, tone of voice, and communication style, you can make them feel more comfortable and understood, increasing their receptivity to your message.

The Principles of Mirroring and Matching

Mirroring and matching involve subtly adjusting your own behavior, body language, and communication style to match those of your prospect. This can create a subconscious sense of similarity and familiarity, making your prospect feel more at ease and open to your message. The key principles of mirroring and matching include:

1. **Body language:** Observe your prospect's posture, gestures,

and facial expressions, and subtly mirror these behaviors to establish rapport.
2. **Tone of voice:** Adjust your tone of voice, speech rate, and volume to match your prospect's, creating a sense of harmony and connection.
3. **Communication style:** Pay attention to your prospect's choice of words, sentence structure, and level of formality, and adjust your own language to align with theirs.

Incorporating Mirroring and Matching in Sales

To effectively use mirroring and matching in your sales approach, consider the following strategies:

- **Be subtle:** Ensure that your mirroring and matching are subtle and natural, as overt or exaggerated mimicry can be off-putting and damage rapport.
- **Observe and adapt:** Continuously observe your prospect's behavior and communication style, and adjust your mirroring and matching as needed throughout the conversation.
- **Be selective:** Focus on mirroring and matching key aspects of your prospect's behavior and communication, rather than attempting to mimic every detail.
- **Maintain authenticity:** Ensure that your mirroring and matching do not compromise your authenticity or sincerity, as this can undermine trust and rapport.

By creating a sense of similarity and familiarity, mirroring and matching can help you establish rapport and connection with your prospects more quickly and effectively. Prospects who feel a strong sense of rapport and connection are more likely to be receptive to your message and open to considering your offering.

3

Chapter 3: Persuasion Techniques

Persuasion is an essential aspect of the sales process, as it enables sales professionals to effectively influence their prospects and guide them toward making a positive decision. Mastering the art of persuasion requires a combination of psychological insights and practical communication skills. In this chapter, we will explore various persuasion techniques that can help sales professionals navigate the complex world of sales and secure more successful outcomes.

The Power of Language

Language is an incredibly powerful tool in the realm of persuasion. The words you choose, the tone you adopt, and the way you structure your sentences can all have a significant impact on how your message is received and perceived by your prospects.

To harness the power of language, use positive and inclusive language that fosters a sense of collaboration and partnership. Focus on the benefits your product or service can provide to your prospect, and paint a vivid picture of the desired outcome. Additionally, be mindful of your tone and ensure that it is warm, engaging, and authentic.

The Art of Asking Questions

Asking questions is an essential skill for sales professionals, as it not only helps to gather valuable information about your prospects but also serves as a powerful persuasion tool. By asking the right questions, you can guide your prospects to reflect on their needs, consider potential solutions, and ultimately, arrive at the conclusion that your product or service is the ideal fit for their requirements.

To master the art of asking questions, focus on open-ended inquiries that encourage your prospects to share their thoughts and feelings. Avoid leading questions that may seem manipulative, and instead, focus on questions that foster reflection and self-discovery.

3.1 The Six Principles of Persuasion

In the world of sales, persuasion is an essential skill for influencing prospects and guiding them toward a buying decision. Dr. Robert Cialdini, a renowned psychologist and expert in the field of persuasion, has identified six universal principles that can be leveraged to increase your persuasive abilities. In this section, we will explore these six principles and provide practical tips for incorporating them into your sales approach.

Dr. Cialdini's six principles of persuasion are:

1. **Reciprocity:** People feel a natural inclination to return favors or kindness. By offering something of value or providing assistance to your prospects, you can create a sense of obligation that may lead to increased cooperation and willingness to engage with your offering.
2. **Commitment and Consistency:** People have a strong desire to appear consistent in their beliefs, attitudes, and behaviors. By encouraging your prospects to make small commitments or statements that align with your offering, you can increase the likelihood that they will follow through with larger commitments or actions.
3. **Social Proof:** People tend to look to others for guidance on how to behave or make decisions, particularly in uncertain situations. Providing testimonials, case studies, or social media endorsements can help demonstrate the value and credibility of your offering, making prospects more likely to trust and engage with your product or service.
4. **Liking:** People are more likely to be influenced by those they like or feel a connection with. Building rapport, finding common ground, and demonstrating genuine interest in your prospects can help increase their receptivity to your message.
5. **Authority:** People tend to trust and respect the opinions of experts or those in positions of authority. Establishing your expertise, sharing relevant credentials, or providing expert endorsements can help enhance your credibility and

influence in the eyes of your prospects.
6. **Scarcity:** People place a higher value on items or opportunities that are perceived to be limited or exclusive. Creating a sense of urgency or exclusivity around your offering can encourage prospects to take action more quickly.

Case Study: The Influence of Scarcity on Consumer Behavior

In a classic study by Worchel, Lee, and Adewole (1975), the researchers examined the effect of scarcity on consumer behavior. They presented participants with two identical jars of cookies – one jar contained ten cookies, while the other contained just two. Despite the cookies being identical, participants consistently rated the cookies from the jar with only two as more valuable and more desirable.

This study demonstrates the power of scarcity in influencing consumer behavior. When a product or service is perceived as scarce or limited, it becomes more attractive to potential buyers. Sales professionals can leverage this psychological principle by emphasizing the limited availability or exclusivity of their offering.

Reference: Worchel, S., Lee, J., & Adewole, A. (1975). Effects of supply and demand on ratings of object value. Journal of Personality and Social Psychology, 32(5), 906-914.

Incorporating the Six Principles of Persuasion in Sales

To leverage Dr. Cialdini's principles of persuasion in your sales approach, consider the following strategies:

- **Offer value upfront:** Provide prospects with valuable information, resources, or assistance early in the sales process to create a sense of reciprocity.
- **Encourage small commitments:** Ask prospects to make small, non-threatening commitments, such as signing up for a newsletter or attending a webinar, to increase their likelihood of making larger commitments later on.
- **Showcase social proof:** Share customer testimonials, case studies, or industry accolades to demonstrate the success and credibility of your product or service.
- **Build rapport and find common ground:** Engage in active listening, show empathy, and identify shared interests or values to create a sense of connection with your prospects.
- **Establish your expertise:** Share your knowledge, experience, and credentials to demonstrate your authority and expertise in your field.
- **Create a sense of urgency:** Use limited-time offers, exclusive promotions, or other scarcity tactics to encourage prospects to take action more quickly.

By understanding and incorporating Dr. Cialdini's six principles of persuasion into your sales approach, you can enhance your ability to influence and guide your prospects toward a buying decision, ultimately increasing your sales success.

3.2 Storytelling: Captivate Your Audience

Storytelling is a powerful tool for sales professionals, as it allows you to engage your prospects on a deeper emotional level, create memorable and impactful messages, and build trust and rapport. By weaving compelling stories into your sales presentations and conversations, you can captivate your audience and make your offering more relatable and persuasive. In this section, we will explore the elements of effective storytelling and provide practical tips for incorporating storytelling into your sales approach.

The Elements of Effective Storytelling

To create engaging and persuasive stories, consider incorporating the following elements:

- **A relatable protagonist:** Your story should feature a protagonist, or main character, who your prospect can identify with or relate to. This could be a real-life customer, a fictional character, or even yourself.
- **A clear narrative structure:** Effective stories follow a clear narrative structure, typically consisting of a beginning, middle, and end. This structure helps guide your audience through the story and makes it easier to follow and understand.
- **Conflict or challenge:** Introduce a conflict, challenge, or problem that the protagonist must overcome. This creates tension and intrigue, making your story more engaging and

emotionally compelling.
- **A resolution or transformation:** Show how the protagonist overcomes the conflict or challenge and experiences a transformation or positive change as a result. This demonstrates the value of your offering and provides a satisfying conclusion to the story.
- **Emotional appeal:** Use vivid descriptions, emotive language, and sensory details to evoke emotions in your audience and create a deeper connection with your story.

Example:

Once upon a time in the quaint town of Springfield, there was a young entrepreneur named Sam who had recently opened his own bakery. Sam was passionate about baking and was known for his delicious and unique creations. However, despite the mouthwatering aroma that filled the air, he had trouble attracting customers to his small bakery.

One day, an older gentleman named Mr. Johnson walked into Sam's bakery. Mr. Johnson was a retired salesman with years of experience in the art of selling. He could see the potential in Sam's bakery and decided to share his wisdom with the young entrepreneur.

"Sam," Mr. Johnson began, "I can see the love and care you put into your baked goods, but you need to give your customers a reason to choose your bakery over the competition."

Sam listened intently as Mr. Johnson shared the elements of effective storytelling in sales. He explained that Sam needed to craft a compelling story that showcased the bakery's unique offerings and connected with customers on an emotional level.

Inspired by Mr. Johnson's advice, Sam began to tell the story of how his grandmother, a skilled baker herself, had passed down her cherished recipes and taught him the importance of using only the finest ingredients. He shared how each delicious pastry was a tribute to his grandmother's love and passion for baking.

As Sam began to weave this heartfelt story into his sales pitch, customers found themselves drawn to his bakery. They felt an emotional connection to Sam's story and his unwavering dedication to his grandmother's legacy. As a result, Sam's bakery began to flourish, with customers lining up each morning to taste the delectable pastries that were made with love.

Through the power of storytelling, Sam was able to transform his small bakery into a thriving business, proving that a compelling story can captivate an audience and leave a lasting impression.

Incorporating Storytelling in Sales

To incorporate storytelling into your sales approach, consider the following strategies:

1. **Share customer success stories:** Use real-life examples of customers who have benefitted from your product or service to demonstrate its value and credibility. Be sure to highlight the challenges they faced, how your offering helped them overcome these challenges, and the positive results they experienced.
2. **Make it personal:** Share your own experiences, challenges, or insights to create a sense of authenticity and connection with your prospects.
3. **Use analogies and metaphors:** Use analogies, metaphors, or vivid imagery to explain complex concepts or ideas in a more engaging and memorable way.
4. **Tailor your stories to your audience:** Customize your stories to address the specific needs, interests, and concerns of your prospects, making them more relevant and impactful.
5. **Practice your storytelling skills:** Like any skill, storytelling requires practice and refinement. Continuously work on improving your storytelling abilities by seeking feedback, observing skilled storytellers, and experimenting with different techniques and approaches.

The Benefits of Storytelling in Sales

Incorporating storytelling into your sales approach can provide numerous benefits, including:

- **Engaging your audience:** Stories can capture your prospect's attention and maintain their interest throughout

your presentation or conversation.
- **Building trust and rapport:** Sharing personal experiences or customer success stories can help create a sense of trust, rapport, and credibility with your prospects.
- **Simplifying complex concepts:** Storytelling can make complex ideas or concepts more accessible and understandable to your audience.
- **Enhancing memorability:** Stories are more likely to be remembered and retained by your prospects, increasing the likelihood that they will recall your message and take action.
- **Influencing decision-making:** By evoking emotions and creating a sense of connection, storytelling can influence your prospect's decision-making process and make your offering more persuasive.

By mastering the art of storytelling and incorporating it into your sales approach, you can captivate your audience, create memorable and impactful messages, and ultimately enhance your influence and sales success.

3.3 Framing: The Art of Contextualizing Your Message

Framing is a powerful communication technique that involves presenting information in a particular context to influence how your audience perceives and interprets your message. By framing your product or service in a manner that highlights its benefits and addresses your prospect's needs, you can create a compelling narrative that resonates with your audience and increases your chances of sales success. In this section, we will explore the principles of framing and provide practical tips for incorporating this technique into your sales approach.

The Principles of Framing

Framing involves presenting information in a specific context, emphasizing certain aspects while downplaying others, to shape your audience's perception of your message. The key principles of framing include:

- **Selective emphasis:** Choose which aspects of your product or service to highlight based on your prospect's needs, preferences, and concerns.
- **Emotional appeal:** Frame your message in a way that evokes emotion, as people are more likely to be influenced by emotional appeals than purely rational arguments.
- **Consistency with values:** Align your message with your prospect's values, beliefs, and priorities to create a sense of congruence and increase receptivity.

Incorporating Framing in Sales

To effectively use framing in your sales approach, consider the following strategies:

1. **Understand your prospect's needs:** Conduct thorough research and engage in active listening to identify your prospect's specific needs, preferences, and concerns. This

information will inform your framing strategy and help you tailor your message accordingly.
2. **Highlight benefits over features:** Frame your product or service in terms of the benefits it provides to your prospect, rather than simply listing its features. Focus on how your offering addresses their needs, solves their problems, or improves their life.
3. **Use positive framing:** Emphasize the positive outcomes or gains that your prospect will experience by choosing your product or service, rather than focusing on the negative consequences of not choosing it.
4. **Leverage social proof:** Frame your offering as a popular, trusted choice by sharing testimonials, case studies, or endorsements from satisfied customers or industry experts.
5. **Create a sense of urgency or exclusivity:** Frame your offering as a limited-time opportunity or an exclusive offer to encourage prospects to take action quickly.
6. **Address objections proactively:** Anticipate potential objections and address them within your framing, demonstrating that you understand and can effectively address your prospect's concerns.

By framing your message in a context that resonates with your prospect, you can increase the persuasive power of your pitch and make your offering more compelling. Aligning your message with your prospect's values, beliefs, and priorities can help establish rapport and trust, increasing their receptivity to your offering. By understanding the principles of framing and incorporating these strategies into your sales approach, you can effectively contextualize your message, resonate with your prospects, and ultimately enhance your influence and sales success.

4

Chapter 4: Overcoming Objections and Resistance

4.1 Identifying and Classifying Objections

In the sales process, objections are inevitable. Prospects may express doubts, concerns, or reservations about your product or service for various reasons. Identifying and classifying these objections is crucial for addressing them effectively and moving your prospect closer to a buying decision. In this chapter, we will explore common types of objections and provide practical tips for recognizing and addressing them in your sales approach.

Common Types of Objections

Objections can be categorized into several common types, each requiring a different approach to address effectively:

- **Price:** Prospects may express concerns about the cost of your product or service or may feel that it is not worth the investment.
- **Need:** Prospects may question the necessity of your product or service, believing that their current solution is sufficient or that they do not require what you are offering.
- **Timing:** Prospects may feel that it is not the right time to make a purchase or may want to delay their decision.
- **Trust:** Prospects may have doubts about the credibility or reliability of your product, service, or company.
- **Compatibility:** Prospects may question whether your product or service aligns with their specific needs, preferences, or existing systems.

Identifying and Addressing Objections

To effectively identify and address objections in your sales approach, consider the following strategies:

1. **Engage in active listening:** Pay close attention to your prospect's words, tone of voice, and body language to pick up on any potential objections or concerns.
2. **Ask open-ended questions:** Encourage your prospect to share their thoughts, feelings, and concerns by asking open-ended questions that invite elaboration.
3. **Anticipate objections:** Based on your research and knowledge of your prospect, try to anticipate potential objections and prepare tailored responses to address them effectively.
4. **Address objections proactively:** Do not wait for your prospect to raise an objection before addressing it. In-

stead, incorporate potential concerns into your sales pitch, demonstrating that you understand and can effectively address their needs.
5. **Remain calm and empathetic:** When faced with an objection, maintain a calm and empathetic demeanor, validating your prospect's concerns and offering solutions without becoming defensive or dismissive.

By mastering the art of identifying and classifying objections, you can better understand your prospect's concerns, address them effectively, and ultimately enhance your influence and sales success. Understanding the root cause of your prospect's objections gives you the ability to present targeted solutions that address their specific concerns and needs.

4.2 Dealing with Resistance: Turning 'No' into 'Yes'

In the sales process, resistance is a natural part of the buyer's journey. Prospects may initially express reluctance or resistance to your offering for various reasons. However, with the right approach, you can transform this resistance into an opportunity to further understand your prospect's needs, address their concerns, and ultimately guide them towards a 'yes.' In this section, we will explore strategies for dealing with resistance and turning initial objections into opportunities for sales success.

Understanding Resistance

Resistance can manifest in various forms during the sales process, including:

- **Skepticism:** Prospects may doubt the value, effectiveness, or credibility of your product or service.
- **Fear of change:** Prospects may be hesitant to adopt a new solution, fearing potential disruptions, costs, or risks associated with change.
- **Inertia:** Prospects may be comfortable with their current solution or situation and unwilling to invest time, energy, or resources into exploring a new alternative.
- **Loyalty:** Prospects may have existing relationships with competitors or other providers and may be reluctant to consider alternative options.

Case Study: The Impact of Emotions on Decision-Making (Bechara et al., 1997)

In 1997, neuroscientist Antoine Bechara and his colleagues conducted a groundbreaking study examining the role of emotions in decision-making. The researchers designed a gambling task known as the Iowa Gambling Task, in which participants were asked to select cards from four decks. Each card resulted in either a gain or a loss, and the goal was to maximize profits. Unbeknownst to the participants, two of the decks were rigged to yield higher overall gains.

The study found that participants began to exhibit emotional responses (as measured by changes in skin conductance) to the high-risk decks before they consciously recognized the pattern. This research revealed that emotions play a crucial role in guiding decision-making, even before conscious awareness kicks in.

This finding has significant implications for sales professionals, as it emphasizes the importance of appealing to emotions when presenting products or services. By creating an emotional connection with prospects, salespeople can influence decision-making and increase the likelihood of a successful sale.

Reference: Bechara, A., Damasio, A. R., Damasio, H., & Anderson, S. W. (1997). Deciding advantageously before knowing the

Strategies for Overcoming Resistance

1. **(When available) Offer a trial or pilot program:** Provide your prospect with the opportunity to test your product or service on a limited basis, reducing the perceived risk and allowing them to experience the benefits firsthand.
2. **Address objections directly:** When faced with resistance, don't shy away from addressing objections head-on. By providing clear and concise responses to your prospects' concerns, you can alleviate their doubts and demonstrate your expertise in the subject matter.
3. **Reframe the conversation:** Sometimes, resistance stems

from a prospect's perspective or the way they perceive the situation. By reframing the conversation and presenting your product or service in a different light, you can help your prospects see the value and benefits more clearly.
4. **Focus on benefits:** Instead of focusing solely on the features of your product or service, emphasize the benefits that your prospects will experience. By highlighting the positive outcomes and the ways in which your offering can improve their lives or solve their problems, you can make it more appealing and reduce resistance.
5. **Practice patience and persistence:** Resistance is a natural part of the sales process, and it's essential to be patient and persistent in your efforts to overcome it. Stay positive, maintain a professional demeanor, and continue to provide valuable information and support to your prospects as they move through the decision-making process.

It takes a lot of learned practical communicative skills to become proficient in overcoming resistance. Remember to not become discouraged, but to try to utilize these critical moments as vital learning experiences to utilize in your future sales calls/meetings. Not every potential lead will buy your product or service no matter how good of a product you have or how amazing you are at selling it. Remain focused, calm, & professional. **Diamonds are formed under pressure.**

> **Example:**
> *Sophia, an experienced sales representative, was pitching a new line of eco-friendly cleaning products to a potential client, Mr. Thompson, the owner of a*

local cleaning company. During their conversation, Mr. Thompson raised an objection about the cost of these eco-friendly products compared to his current, traditional cleaning supplies.

"Your products sound great, Sophia," said Mr. Thompson, "but they are significantly more expensive than the ones we currently use. I'm not sure I can justify the increased expense."

Sophia, well-prepared for this objection, responded confidently, "I understand your concern, Mr. Thompson. However, I'd like to share some information that might change your perspective."

She continued, "While it's true that our eco-friendly products are slightly more expensive upfront, they offer several long-term benefits that can save your company money in the long run. For instance, our products are highly concentrated, which means you'll use less product per cleaning job. This will lower your overall costs and reduce the frequency of reordering supplies."

Sophia went on to explain the environmental benefits of switching to eco-friendly products, including reduced plastic waste and a decrease in harmful chemicals being released into the environment. She also pointed out the positive impact that switching to eco-friendly products could have on Mr. Thompson's company's image.

"More and more consumers are becoming environmentally conscious, Mr. Thompson. By switching to eco-friendly products, you'll demonstrate to your customers that you care about the environment, and this could lead to increased customer loyalty and potentially attract new clients."

Mr. Thompson, now considering the long-term benefits and potential to attract new customers, started to see the value of investing in eco-friendly cleaning products. Sophia's ability to address his objection by reframing the issue and highlighting the long-term benefits helped her successfully overcome Mr. Thompson's initial resistance.

5

Chapter 5: Closing the Deal

Closing the deal is the culmination of your efforts in the sales process. It's the moment when your prospect decides to commit to your product or service, and you successfully convert them into a customer. Mastering the art of closing requires a combination of effective communication, empathy, and timing. In this chapter, we will explore various closing techniques and provide practical tips for successfully closing the deal.

Closing Techniques

There are several closing techniques that can be employed depending on the specific needs of your prospect and the nature of your sales process:

- **Assumptive Close:** This technique involves acting as if the prospect has already decided to buy your product or service. You might start discussing the next steps, such as implementation or payment plans, assuming that the

prospect has agreed to move forward.
- **Summary Close:** Summarize the key benefits and features of your product or service that address your prospect's needs, reiterating the value proposition and emphasizing the reasons why they should choose your offering.
- **Urgency Close:** Create a sense of urgency by emphasizing the limited availability of your product or service, or by offering a special promotion or discount for a limited time.
- **Question Close:** Ask your prospect a question that encourages them to make a decision, such as "Are you ready to move forward with this solution?" or "Do you think this product will address your needs?"
- **Trial Close:** Test your prospect's readiness to commit by asking a less intimidating question, such as "How do you feel about the solution we've discussed?" or "What are your thoughts on the proposed plan?"

Case Study: The Foot-in-the-Door Technique (Freedman & Fraser, 1966)

A classic study conducted by Jonathan Freedman and Scott Fraser in 1966 examined the effectiveness of the foot-in-the-door technique, a sales strategy that involves making a small initial request followed by a larger, more significant request. In their study, the researchers approached homeowners and asked them to display a small sign supporting safe driving in their front yard. Two weeks later, they returned and asked the same homeowners to display a larger, more obtrusive sign with the same message.

> *The results showed that 76% of those who agreed to display the small sign were willing to display the larger sign, compared to only 17% of homeowners who had not been approached with the initial request. This research supports the foot-in-the-door technique as an effective sales strategy, demonstrating that obtaining an initial small commitment can increase the likelihood of prospects agreeing to larger requests.*
>
> *Reference: Freedman, J. L., & Fraser, S. C. (1966). Compliance without pressure: The foot-in-the-door technique. Journal of Personality and Social Psychology, 4(2), 195-202.*

Tips for Successfully Closing the Deal

To effectively close the deal, consider the following strategies:

- **Read your prospect's cues:** Pay close attention to your prospect's verbal and non-verbal cues, such as their tone of voice, body language, and expressions. This will help you gauge their level of interest and readiness to commit.
- **Address any lingering objections:** Ensure that you have addressed all of your prospect's concerns and objections before attempting to close the deal. This may involve revisiting certain points, providing additional information, or offering reassurance.
- **Choose the right closing technique:** Select a closing technique that aligns with your prospect's needs and prefer-

ences, as well as the nature of your sales process.
- **Be confident and assertive:** Display confidence in your product or service and its ability to address your prospect's needs, while maintaining a respectful and assertive demeanor.
- **Know when to walk away:** Recognize when a prospect is not a good fit for your product or service, or when they are not ready to commit. In these situations, it may be more beneficial to part ways amicably and revisit the opportunity at a later time.

The Benefits of Mastering the Art of Closing

Successfully closing deals can provide several benefits for sales professionals, including:

1. **Increased sales success:** By mastering the art of closing, you can convert more prospects into customers, ultimately driving sales growth and success.
2. **Enhanced customer satisfaction:** Successfully addressing your prospect's needs and concerns throughout the sales process can lead to increased customer satisfaction and loyalty.
3. **Greater confidence and assertiveness:** As you develop your closing skills, you will become more confident and assertive in your sales approach, leading to better overall performance.

By understanding and incorporating various closing techniques and strategies into your sales approach, you can effectively guide your prospects towards a buying decision and ultimately master the art of closing the deal.

Negotiation Techniques for Sales Success

Negotiation is a critical aspect of the sales process, as it often determines the terms and conditions under which a deal is closed. Mastering the art of negotiation can significantly improve your sales success, enabling you to secure favorable terms and conditions for both you and your client. In this section, we will explore various negotiation techniques and provide practical tips for achieving sales success through effective negotiation.

Principles of Negotiation

Successful negotiation relies on several key principles, including:

- **Preparation:** Thoroughly research and understand your prospect's needs, priorities, and constraints before entering into negotiations.
- **Win-win mindset:** Approach negotiations with the goal of achieving a mutually beneficial outcome that addresses both parties' needs and interests.
- **Flexibility:** Be open to compromise and willing to adjust your position or offer in response to your prospect's needs and concerns.
- **Persistence:** Remain steadfast in your pursuit of a favorable outcome, even in the face of challenges or setbacks.

CHAPTER 5: CLOSING THE DEAL

Negotiation Techniques for Sales Success

To effectively negotiate in your sales approach, consider the following strategies:

1. **Set clear objectives:** Clearly define your goals and desired outcomes for the negotiation, ensuring that they align with your prospect's needs and interests.
2. **Identify your BATNA (Best Alternative to a Negotiated Agreement):** Understand your best alternative option if the negotiation fails, which will help you determine your limits and leverage in the negotiation process.
3. **Establish your value proposition:** Clearly articulate the benefits and value that your product or service offers, demonstrating how it addresses your prospect's needs and priorities.
4. **Offer concessions strategically:** Be willing to make concessions, but do so strategically, ensuring that you receive something in return for each concession you make.
5. **Maintain a collaborative mindset:** Focus on finding common ground and developing solutions that address both parties' needs and interests, rather than engaging in a confrontational or adversarial approach.

The Benefits of Effective Negotiation

Mastering the art of negotiation can provide several benefits for sales professionals, including:

1. **Increased sales success:** By securing favorable terms and

conditions, you can close more deals and achieve greater sales success.
2. **Enhanced customer satisfaction:** Successfully addressing your prospect's needs and concerns through negotiation can lead to increased customer satisfaction and loyalty.
3. **Improved relationships:** A collaborative, win-win approach to negotiation can strengthen your relationships with prospects and clients, fostering trust and rapport.

By understanding the principles of negotiation and incorporating effective negotiation techniques into your sales approach, you can achieve greater success in closing deals and ultimately mastering the art of influence.

6

Chapter 6: The Salesperson's Mindset

A salesperson's mindset plays a crucial role in their overall success. The way sales professionals view themselves, their prospects, and the sales process can significantly impact their ability to establish connections, build trust, and ultimately close deals. In this chapter, we will explore the key components of a successful salesperson's mindset and discuss strategies for cultivating a mental framework that fosters growth and achievement in the world of sales.

Embracing a Growth Mindset

A growth mindset is the belief that one's abilities and intelligence can be developed and improved through hard work, dedication, and learning. This mindset is in stark contrast to a fixed mindset, where individuals believe that their abilities and intelligence are static and cannot be changed.

By embracing a growth mindset, sales professionals can remain open to learning, adapt to challenges, and continuously work to improve their skills. To cultivate a growth mindset, focus on setting realistic yet ambitious goals, seeking constructive feedback, and embracing challenges as opportunities for growth.

Adopting a Customer-Centric Focus

A customer-centric mindset places the needs, desires, and experiences of your prospects at the center of your sales approach. This perspective enables you to better understand your prospects and tailor your sales interactions to address their unique concerns and motivations.

To adopt a customer-centric focus, prioritize empathy and active listening during your sales interactions. Make a conscious effort to see the world through your prospects' eyes, and strive to provide solutions that genuinely meet their needs.

Fostering a Positive Attitude

A positive attitude can have a powerful impact on your sales success. By maintaining an optimistic and resilient outlook, you can navigate the inevitable ups and downs of the sales process with greater ease and stay motivated in the face of adversity.

To foster a positive attitude, practice gratitude, and focus on the aspects of your sales role that you genuinely enjoy. Additionally, surround yourself with supportive colleagues and mentors who can offer encouragement and guidance when needed.

Developing Self-Confidence

Self-confidence is an essential attribute for sales professionals, as it enables them to communicate effectively, build trust with prospects, and convey the value of their products or services. By cultivating self-confidence, you can more effectively navigate the sales process and present yourself as a knowledgeable, trustworthy partner to your prospects.

To develop self-confidence, focus on building your expertise in your industry and product offerings. Additionally, practice positive self-talk and remind yourself of your past successes and achievements to reinforce your belief in your abilities.

Embracing Adaptability

The world of sales is constantly evolving, and sales professionals must be able to adapt to changes in their industry, market, and customer expectations. By embracing adaptability, you can stay ahead of the curve and ensure that your sales approach remains relevant and effective.

To cultivate adaptability, remain open to learning and seeking new information. Stay current with industry trends and developments, and be willing to adjust your sales strategies and techniques as needed to meet the changing needs of your prospects.

6.1 Building Resilience: Overcoming Rejection and Failure

Rejection and failure are inevitable aspects of the sales profession. However, it's not the setbacks themselves that determine your success but how you respond to them. Building resilience is crucial for overcoming rejection and failure, learning from these experiences, and moving forward with a positive mindset. In this section, we will explore strategies for building resilience and effectively managing rejection and failure in the sales process.

Understanding Rejection and Failure

Rejection and failure can manifest in various forms throughout the sales process, including:

1. **Lost sales opportunities:** Failing to close a deal or losing a prospect to a competitor.
2. **Unmet goals:** Falling short of your personal or professional sales targets.
3. **Negative feedback:** Receiving criticism or negative feedback from prospects, clients, or colleagues.
4. **Mistakes or errors:** Making mistakes in your sales approach or strategy.

Strategies for Building Resilience

To build resilience and effectively manage rejection and failure, consider the following strategies:

- **Cultivate a growth mindset:** Embrace challenges and setbacks as opportunities for learning and growth, rather than viewing them as definitive measures of your worth or ability.
- **Reframe negative experiences:** Shift your perspective on rejection and failure, focusing on the lessons learned and opportunities for improvement.
- **Set realistic expectations:** Recognize that rejection and failure are natural aspects of the sales process and set realistic expectations for your performance.
- **Develop a support network:** Surround yourself with supportive colleagues, friends, and mentors who can offer encouragement, guidance, and perspective during challenging times.
- **Practice self-compassion:** Treat yourself with kindness and understanding when faced with setbacks, recognizing that everyone experiences rejection and failure at times.
- **Focus on your accomplishments:** Regularly acknowledge and celebrate your achievements, both large and small, to maintain a balanced perspective on your overall performance.
- **Develop effective coping strategies:** Learn and practice healthy coping mechanisms, such as exercise, meditation, or journaling, to help manage stress and maintain a positive mindset.

The Benefits of Building Resilience

Cultivating resilience can provide several benefits for sales professionals, including:

1. Improved performance: By effectively managing rejection and failure, you can maintain a positive mindset and stay focused on your goals, ultimately leading to better overall performance.
2. Increased adaptability: Resilience enables you to adapt and respond effectively to challenges and setbacks, allowing you to continually evolve and improve your sales approach.
3. Enhanced well-being: Developing resilience can help mitigate the negative effects of stress, burnout, and self-doubt, leading to improved mental and emotional well-being.

By embracing a growth mindset, reframing negative experiences, and practicing effective coping strategies, you can build resilience and successfully navigate the challenges and setbacks inherent in the sales profession. Ultimately, cultivating resilience will empower you to overcome rejection and failure, continually grow and improve, and master the art of influence.

6.2 Goal Setting and Motivation

Goal setting and motivation are essential components of success in the sales profession. By setting clear, achievable goals and maintaining the motivation to pursue them, you can drive your performance, increase your sales success, and continually grow and develop as a sales professional. In this section, we will explore the importance of goal setting and motivation, and provide practical strategies for setting and pursuing your sales goals.

The Importance of Goal Setting and Motivation

Goal setting and motivation play a crucial role in the sales profession for several reasons:

1. **Clarity and focus:** Setting specific, measurable goals provides you with a clear direction and helps you maintain focus on your priorities.
2. **Performance measurement:** Goals enable you to track your progress and evaluate your performance, allowing you to identify areas for improvement and celebrate your successes.
3. **Personal and professional growth:** Pursuing ambitious goals encourages you to continually develop your skills, knowledge, and capabilities, ultimately driving personal and professional growth.
4. **Increased motivation and engagement:** Setting and working towards meaningful goals can increase your motivation and engagement in your work, leading to higher levels of satisfaction and success.

Strategies for Effective Goal Setting and Motivation

To set and pursue effective sales goals, consider the following strategies:

- **Set SMART goals:** Ensure that your goals are Specific, Measurable, Achievable, Relevant, and Time-bound, providing you with a clear roadmap for success.
- **Break down larger goals:** Break larger, long-term goals into smaller, more manageable short-term objectives, making it easier to maintain momentum and motivation.
- **Develop an action plan:** Create a detailed action plan that outlines the steps and resources needed to achieve your goals, ensuring that you have a clear path forward.
- **Monitor your progress:** Regularly track and evaluate your progress towards your goals, adjusting your approach or objectives as needed to stay on track.
- **Stay accountable:** Share your goals with a trusted colleague, mentor, or friend, who can provide support, encouragement, and accountability.
- **Stay motivated:** Find sources of motivation and inspiration that resonate with you, such as success stories, motivational quotes, or personal development resources.
- **Celebrate your successes:** Acknowledge and celebrate your achievements, both large and small, to maintain a positive mindset and stay motivated in the pursuit of your goals.

The Benefits of Goal Setting and Motivation

By setting and pursuing effective sales goals, you can enjoy several benefits, including:

1. **Increased sales success:** Goal setting and motivation can drive your performance and help you achieve greater sales success.

2. **Enhanced personal and professional growth:** Pursuing ambitious goals can lead to continual development and growth in your skills, knowledge, and capabilities.
3. **Greater job satisfaction:** Working towards meaningful goals can increase your engagement and satisfaction in your work, leading to higher levels of overall job satisfaction.

By mastering the art of goal setting and motivation, you can create a clear roadmap for success, drive your performance, and ultimately achieve your full potential in the sales profession.

6.3 Continuous Learning and Self-Improvement

In the ever-evolving world of sales, continuous learning and self-improvement are essential for staying ahead of the curve and maintaining a competitive edge. By committing to lifelong learning and personal growth, you can enhance your skills, expand your knowledge, and continually refine your sales approach. In this section, we will explore the importance of continuous learning and self-improvement, and provide practical strategies for fostering a lifelong learning mindset in your sales career.

The Importance of Continuous Learning and Self-Improvement

Continuous learning and self-improvement are vital in the sales profession for several reasons:

1. **Adaptability:** The sales landscape is constantly changing, with new technologies, trends, and strategies continually emerging. Continuous learning enables you to stay current and adapt to these changes effectively.
2. **Competitive advantage:** By continually expanding your knowledge and skills, you can maintain a competitive edge in the market and enhance your value proposition to prospects and clients.
3. **Personal and professional growth:** A commitment to learning and growth can lead to increased satisfaction, motivation, and success in your sales career.

Strategies for Fostering Continuous Learning and Self-Improvement

To cultivate a mindset of continuous learning and self-improvement, consider the following strategies:

- **Set learning goals:** Establish specific, measurable learning goals that align with your personal and professional objectives, and create an action plan to achieve them.
- **Seek out educational opportunities:** Pursue formal and informal learning opportunities, such as workshops, conferences, online courses, and books, to expand your knowledge and skills.
- **Learn from others:** Network with other sales professionals, join industry groups, and seek out mentors to gain insights, share experiences, and learn from others in your field.
- **Embrace feedback:** Solicit constructive feedback from col-

leagues, clients, and mentors, and use this feedback to identify areas for improvement and growth.
- **Reflect on your experiences:** Regularly reflect on your successes, failures, and lessons learned, using these insights to inform your future growth and development.
- **Stay curious:** Cultivate a curious mindset, asking questions, seeking out new perspectives, and challenging your assumptions to foster a continuous learning mentality.
- **Be persistent:** Recognize that learning and growth are ongoing processes, and remain committed to your development, even in the face of setbacks or challenges.

The Benefits of Continuous Learning and Self-Improvement

By embracing a mindset of continuous learning and self-improvement, you can enjoy several benefits, including:

1. **Enhanced performance:** Continually expanding your skills and knowledge can lead to improved sales performance and increased success.
2. **Increased adaptability:** Continuous learning enables you to effectively navigate changes in the sales landscape, ensuring that your approach remains relevant and effective.
3. **Personal and professional growth:** A commitment to learning and growth can foster increased satisfaction, motivation, and success in your sales career.

By prioritizing continuous learning and self-improvement, you can stay ahead of the curve, continually refine your sales approach, and ultimately master the art of influence in the ever-changing world of sales.

Chapter 7: Advanced Sales Techniques

In the competitive world of sales, it is essential for professionals to continually refine their skills and explore new techniques to stay ahead of the curve. The previous chapters of this book have laid the foundation for understanding the fundamental principles of selling and the psychological aspects that influence the decision-making process. Now, it's time to take your sales prowess to the next level by delving into advanced sales techniques that can truly set you apart from the competition.

The importance of utilizing advanced sales techniques cannot be overstated. As markets become more saturated and customers grow more discerning, sales professionals must be able to differentiate themselves and their offerings in order to secure a competitive edge. Advanced sales techniques allow you to build stronger relationships with your prospects, tailor your approach to their unique needs and preferences, and ultimately, close more deals.

In this chapter, we will explore a variety of advanced sales techniques, including consultative selling, value-based selling, solution selling, and more. We will also examine case studies that demonstrate the real-world effectiveness of these approaches. By the end of this chapter, you will be equipped with a comprehensive toolkit of advanced sales techniques that can help you elevate your sales game and achieve greater success in your career.

Solution Selling

Solution selling is a sales approach that focuses on addressing the specific needs and pain points of your prospect rather than merely pushing a product or service. The key to solution selling is understanding your prospects' unique challenges and presenting your offering as the ideal solution to those challenges.

> **Case Study:**
>
> *A software company was struggling to sell their Customer Relationship Management (CRM) system to businesses in a highly competitive market. Instead of focusing on the system's features, their sales team decided to adopt a solution selling approach. They conducted extensive research on their prospects' industries and identified common pain points such as disjointed communication, inefficient processes, and lost sales opportunities. By presenting their CRM as the ideal solution to these challenges, the software company was able to increase sales by 30% within six months.*

Value-based Selling

Value-based selling is a sales approach that emphasizes the value your product or service can bring to the prospect, rather than focusing solely on price. This method requires a deep understanding of your offering's unique value proposition and the ability to communicate that value in a compelling way.

> **Case Study:**
>
> *A company selling high-end kitchen appliances was struggling to compete with lower-priced competitors. By adopting a value-based selling approach, their sales team began to emphasize the long-term savings and benefits of investing in their high-quality appliances. They highlighted the appliances' energy efficiency, durability, and advanced features that could save customers time and effort in the kitchen. As a result, the company saw a significant increase in sales, with customers willing to pay a premium for the added value their products provided.*

Challenger Sales Approach

The Challenger sales approach, based on the book "The Challenger Sale" by Matthew Dixon and Brent Adamson, is a sales technique that focuses on challenging your prospects' assumptions and beliefs. Instead of building rapport by agreeing with the prospect, the Challenger salesperson actively questions their beliefs, pushing them to think differently and consider new solutions.

Case Study:

A marketing agency was struggling to convince prospects of the value of their comprehensive digital marketing services. By adopting the Challenger sales approach, their sales team began to question prospects' assumptions about the effectiveness of their current marketing strategies. By challenging their beliefs and presenting new data and insights, the agency was able to demonstrate the value of their services and increase their client base.

SPIN Selling

SPIN selling, a technique developed by Neil Rackham, is an acronym for Situation, Problem, Implication, and Need-Payoff. This approach involves asking a series of questions that guide the prospect through a process of identifying their current situation, uncovering problems, understanding the implications of those problems, and ultimately discovering the value of the solution you're offering.

Case Study:

A sales representative for a medical equipment company used the SPIN selling technique to secure a large contract with a hospital. The representative first asked questions to understand the hospital's current situation, then guided the conversation towards the problems they were facing, such as outdated equipment and long patient wait times. By discussing the implications of these problems, the representative was able to demonstrate the need for the company's advanced medical equipment and secure the contract.

Consultative Selling

Consultative selling focuses on building relationships with your prospects and understanding their needs, rather than merely pitching a product or service. This approach involves asking open-ended questions to gain insight into your prospects' problems and pain points. By actively listening and demonstrating empathy, you can position yourself as a trusted advisor who genuinely cares about helping them find the right solution.

Case Study: The Success of Consultative Selling in the Software Industry

A leading software company decided to implement a consultative selling approach to improve their sales performance. They trained their sales team to focus on understanding the prospects' business challenges and tailoring their presentations accordingly. As a result, the sales team was able to better address the prospects' concerns and demonstrate the value of their software solutions in solving those problems. Over the course of a year, the company saw a 35% increase in sales, proving the effectiveness of the consultative selling approach.

Strategic Account Management

Strategic account management involves developing long-term relationships with your key clients and working closely with them to identify new business opportunities. This approach requires a deep understanding of your clients' needs and objectives, as well as the ability to align your product or service offerings with their strategic goals.

> ### Case Study: An Insurance Company's Success with Strategic Account Management
> *An insurance company decided to implement a strategic account management program to strengthen relationships with its top clients. The company assigned dedicated account managers to each key client, who worked closely with them to understand their evolving needs and identify new sales opportunities. Over the course of two years, the company saw a 30% increase in revenue from its key clients, demonstrating the power of strategic account management.*

Chapter 8: Digital Sales and the Future of Selling

As technology continues to evolve and shape the way we conduct business, the sales landscape has transformed dramatically. Digital sales have become an integral aspect of modern selling, requiring sales professionals to adapt their approach and leverage technology to better connect with prospects, enhance their value proposition, and ultimately close more deals. In this chapter, we will explore the world of digital sales and discuss how to harness the power of technology to excel in the future of selling.

The Rise of Digital Sales

The digital revolution has had a profound impact on the sales profession. With the rise of the internet, social media, and e-commerce platforms, the way we buy and sell goods and services has been transformed. As a result, sales professionals must embrace new technologies and develop new skills to remain competitive in the digital age.

One of the most significant changes in the sales landscape is the shift from traditional face-to-face selling to digital sales channels. Today, prospects and customers can research, compare, and purchase products and services online, often without ever interacting with a salesperson. This has led to a growing emphasis on inbound marketing, content creation, and social selling, as sales professionals seek to engage and influence prospects through digital channels.

Adapting to the Digital Sales Landscape

To thrive in the digital age, sales professionals must adapt their approach and develop new skills to engage and influence prospects effectively. Some key strategies for adapting to the digital sales landscape include:

- **Embrace social selling:** Social selling involves leveraging social media platforms to build relationships, share valuable content, and engage with prospects and customers. By cultivating a strong online presence and becoming a trusted resource, sales professionals can expand their reach and influence in the digital space.
- **Develop digital communication skills:** As more sales interactions take place through digital channels, sales professionals must develop strong digital communication skills. This includes writing compelling emails, engaging in live chat conversations, and conducting video calls, all while maintaining a personal and authentic connection.

- **Leverage data and analytics:** Digital sales channels generate a wealth of data that can be used to inform and refine your sales approach. By leveraging data and analytics, sales professionals can better understand their prospects' behavior, preferences, and needs, enabling them to deliver more targeted and effective sales messages.
- **Invest in sales technology:** Sales technology, such as customer relationship management (CRM) systems, marketing automation tools, and sales enablement platforms, can help sales professionals streamline their processes, enhance their productivity, and deliver a more personalized and engaging experience to prospects.

The Future of Selling

As the digital revolution continues to unfold, the future of selling will be shaped by several key trends and developments, including:

1. **Artificial intelligence (AI) and machine learning:** AI and machine learning technologies have the potential to revolutionize the sales profession by automating routine tasks, personalizing customer interactions, and providing valuable insights to drive sales performance.
2. **Virtual and augmented reality:** Virtual and augmented reality technologies can create immersive, interactive experiences that enable sales professionals to showcase their products and services in new and engaging ways.
3. **The rise of remote selling:** With the increasing prevalence of remote work, sales professionals will need to master the

art of virtual selling, as face-to-face interactions become less common and digital channels continue to grow in importance.
4. **The importance of customer experience:** As competition intensifies in the digital age, delivering a seamless, personalized customer experience will become increasingly critical to sales success.

By embracing digital sales, honing new skills, and staying abreast of emerging trends and technologies, sales professionals can successfully navigate the future of selling and continue to master the art of influence in the digital age.

8.1 The Power of Social Media and Content Marketing

In today's digital age, the sales landscape has expanded far beyond traditional face-to-face interactions. Social media and content marketing have emerged as powerful tools for sales professionals, enabling them to reach and engage with a broader audience, build trust and credibility, and ultimately drive sales success. In this section, we will explore the importance of social media and content marketing in the modern sales process and provide practical strategies for leveraging these tools to enhance your sales efforts.

The Role of Social Media and Content Marketing in Sales

Social media and content marketing play a crucial role in the sales process by providing sales professionals with new ways to connect with prospects, demonstrate their expertise, and establish trust. By sharing valuable content and engaging in meaningful conversations on social media, sales professionals can expand their reach, enhance their credibility, and ultimately influence the buying decisions of their target audience.

Strategies for Effective Social Media and Content Marketing

To leverage social media and content marketing effectively in your sales efforts, consider the following strategies:

- **Choose the right platforms:** Focus your efforts on the social media platforms most relevant to your target audience and industry. This may include platforms such as LinkedIn, Twitter, Facebook, or Instagram, depending on your specific niche.
- **Develop a consistent brand presence:** Create a cohesive and professional brand presence across your social media profiles, ensuring that your messaging, imagery, and tone are consistent with your personal or company brand.
- **Share valuable content:** Develop and share content that is relevant, valuable, and engaging to your target audience. This may include blog posts, articles, videos, infographics, or podcasts that address common challenges, offer expert insights, or provide practical tips and advice.
- **Engage with your audience:** Foster genuine connections with your audience by responding to comments, answering questions, and participating in conversations on social me-

dia. By engaging in authentic and meaningful interactions, you can build trust and credibility with your prospects.
- **Leverage social listening:** Monitor social media conversations and trends to identify opportunities for engagement, gather insights about your target audience, and stay informed about industry developments.
- **Collaborate with influencers:** Partner with industry influencers or thought leaders to co-create content, expand your reach, and enhance your credibility in the eyes of your target audience.
- **Measure your results:** Track your social media and content marketing efforts to determine their effectiveness, and adjust your strategy as needed to maximize your impact.

The Benefits of Social Media and Content Marketing in Sales

By effectively leveraging social media and content marketing, sales professionals can enjoy several benefits, including:

1. **Expanded reach:** Social media and content marketing can significantly expand your reach, enabling you to connect with a larger audience of potential prospects.
2. **Enhanced credibility:** Sharing valuable content and engaging in meaningful conversations on social media can help to establish your credibility and expertise in the eyes of your target audience.
3. **Stronger relationships:** By fostering genuine connections and providing value through content and social media interactions, you can build stronger relationships with your prospects, enhancing their trust and loyalty.

4. **Increased sales success:** Ultimately, leveraging the power of social media and content marketing can help to influence the buying decisions of your target audience, driving sales success.

By mastering the art of social media and content marketing, sales professionals can harness the power of the digital landscape to expand their reach, build trust and credibility, and ultimately drive sales success in the modern sales environment.

8.2 Email Marketing: Crafting Compelling Sales Messages

In today's digital age, email remains a powerful and effective tool for sales professionals to reach and engage with their prospects. A well-crafted email can convey your value proposition, establish trust, and ultimately, influence the recipient's buying decisions. In this section, we will explore the principles of effective email marketing and provide practical tips for crafting compelling sales messages that resonate with your target audience.

The Importance of Email Marketing in Sales

Despite the rise of social media and other digital communication channels, email marketing continues to play a crucial role in the sales process. Some key reasons for the enduring importance of email marketing include:

1. **Wide reach:** With billions of active email users worldwide, email marketing offers an unparalleled opportunity to connect with a large and diverse audience.
2. **Personalization:** Email enables sales professionals to deliver personalized, targeted messages that cater to the specific needs and interests of individual prospects.
3. **Relationship building:** By consistently delivering valuable content and engaging in meaningful conversations via email, sales professionals can build and nurture relationships with their prospects, fostering trust and loyalty over time.

Strategies for Crafting Compelling Sales Emails

To create persuasive and engaging sales emails, consider the following strategies:

- **Focus on your subject line:** Your subject line is the first thing your recipient sees, and it plays a critical role in determining whether your email gets opened. To increase open rates, craft a subject line that is compelling, relevant, and concise.
- **Personalize your message:** Tailor your email to the recipient's needs, interests, and preferences. Use their name, reference specific details about their situation or previous interactions, and demonstrate that you understand their unique challenges or goals.
- **Clearly communicate your value proposition:** Clearly artic-

ulate the benefits of your product or service, and explain how it can solve the recipient's problem or help them achieve their goals.
- **Use persuasive language:** Leverage persuasive techniques such as storytelling, social proof, and scarcity to make your message more compelling and convincing.
- **Be concise and scannable:** Keep your email brief and to the point, and use formatting elements such as headings, bullet points, and bold text to make it easy for the reader to quickly scan and understand your message.
- **Include a clear call-to-action (CTA):** Clearly state the action you want the recipient to take, whether it's to schedule a call, download a resource, or make a purchase. Ensure that your CTA is prominent and easy to locate within the email.
- **Optimize for mobile:** With more people accessing their email on mobile devices, it's essential to ensure that your email is mobile-friendly and easy to read on smaller screens.

Measuring and Improving Your Email Marketing Success

To maximize the effectiveness of your email marketing efforts, it's important to measure your results and continually refine your approach. Key metrics to track include open rates, click-through rates, and conversion rates. Analyze these metrics to identify trends, areas for improvement, and best practices that resonate with your audience.

By continually testing and optimizing your email marketing strategy, you can enhance your ability to craft compelling sales messages that resonate with your target audience, build trust, and ultimately drive sales success.

In conclusion, email marketing remains a powerful tool for sales professionals to connect with prospects, communicate their value proposition, and influence buying decisions. By mastering the art of crafting compelling sales emails, you can leverage the power of email marketing to enhance your sales efforts and achieve greater success in the digital age.

8.3 The Role of Artificial Intelligence in Sales

The rapid advancement of technology has begun to reshape the landscape of sales, and artificial intelligence (AI) is at the forefront of this transformation. AI technologies have the potential to revolutionize the way sales professionals approach their work by automating repetitive tasks, personalizing customer interactions, and providing valuable insights to optimize sales performance. In this section, we will explore the role of artificial intelligence in sales and discuss how sales professionals can leverage AI to enhance their skills and achieve greater success.

Understanding Artificial Intelligence in Sales

Artificial intelligence refers to the development of computer systems capable of performing tasks that typically require human intelligence. In the context of sales, AI technologies can be used to analyze large amounts of data, recognize patterns, make predictions, and automate various aspects of the sales process.

AI-powered tools and platforms can help sales professionals become more efficient, make better decisions, and provide a more personalized experience to their customers. By harnessing the power of AI, sales professionals can focus on higher-value tasks, such as building relationships and closing deals, while relying on AI to handle time-consuming and mundane tasks.

The Applications of AI in Sales

AI technologies can be applied to various aspects of the sales process, including lead generation, lead scoring, customer relationship management (CRM), and sales forecasting. Some key applications of AI in sales include:

1. **Lead generation and scoring:** AI can analyze large volumes of data to identify and prioritize high-quality leads. By using machine learning algorithms, AI can recognize patterns in customer behavior and preferences, helping sales professionals target the most promising prospects.
2. **CRM automation:** AI-powered CRM systems can streamline various aspects of customer relationship management, such as data entry, contact management, and task scheduling. This allows sales professionals to spend more time on high-value tasks, such as engaging with prospects and closing deals.
3. **Sales forecasting:** AI can analyze historical sales data and market trends to predict future sales performance. These

insights can help sales professionals make more informed decisions about their sales strategy and resource allocation.

4. **Personalized customer interactions:** AI technologies can help sales professionals deliver more personalized and relevant experiences to their customers. For example, AI-powered chatbots can handle routine customer inquiries and provide tailored product recommendations based on customer preferences and behavior.

Artificial intelligence has the potential to revolutionize the sales industry by automating tasks, personalizing customer interactions, and providing valuable insights. By embracing the advancement of technology, you can outperform your competitors, obtain more customers & increase your sales!

Chapter 9: Building A Successful Marketing Campaign

A successful marketing campaign is the cornerstone of any thriving sales strategy. By creating a compelling message that resonates with your target audience, you can generate interest, build brand awareness, and ultimately, drive sales. In this chapter, we'll explore the key components of an effective marketing campaign utilizing different ad strategies and discuss how to leverage the principles of psychology to maximize its impact.

Define Your Objectives and Target Audience

The first step in building a successful marketing campaign is to clearly define your objectives and target audience. What are your goals for the campaign, and who are you trying to reach? By honing in on specific objectives and identifying your ideal customer, you can create a focused and relevant message that resonates with your audience.

Craft a Compelling Message

The heart of any marketing campaign is the message you communicate to your audience. To create a compelling message, consider the unique selling points of your product or service, and how they address the needs, desires, and pain points of your target audience. Use storytelling techniques to create an emotional connection and make your message memorable.

Leverage the Power of Emotions

As discussed in the previous chapters, emotions play a significant role in decision-making. To maximize the effectiveness of your marketing campaign, tap into the emotions that drive your target audience. Consider the fears, desires, and aspirations that motivate them, and craft a message that evokes these emotions.

Apply the Principles of Persuasion

To influence your audience and encourage them to take action, incorporate the principles of persuasion discussed in earlier chapters, such as social proof, scarcity, and reciprocity. By using these proven techniques, you can enhance the persuasiveness of your marketing campaign and improve your chances of driving sales.

Choose the Right Channels

To reach your target audience, it's essential to select the most appropriate marketing channels. Consider the demographics, interests, and media consumption habits of your audience when choosing the best platforms for your campaign. A combination of traditional and digital channels, such as print, television, social media, and content marketing, may be most effective in reaching a diverse audience.

Create a Consistent Brand Image

A consistent brand image is crucial for building trust and recognition among your audience. Ensure that your marketing campaign aligns with your overall brand identity, including your visual branding, tone of voice, and messaging. This consistency will help to create a cohesive customer experience and reinforce your brand values.

Test and Optimize

No marketing campaign is perfect from the outset. To maximize your chances of success, it's crucial to test and optimize your campaign based on data and feedback from your audience. Analyze the performance of your campaign across various channels, identify areas of improvement, and make the necessary adjustments to enhance its effectiveness.

Measure Your Success

Finally, it's essential to measure the success of your marketing campaign by tracking key performance indicators (KPIs) that align with your objectives. This data will help you determine the return on investment (ROI) of your campaign, allowing you to make informed decisions about future marketing initiatives.

Building a successful marketing campaign requires a deep understanding of your target audience, a compelling message, and the effective application of psychological principles. By incorporating these elements into your campaign, you can create a powerful marketing strategy that supports your sales efforts and drives your business toward success.

Case Study: Dove's "Real Beauty" Campaign

In 2004, Dove launched its groundbreaking "Real Beauty" campaign, which aimed to challenge the traditional beauty standards perpetuated by the media and celebrate the diverse beauty of women worldwide (Edelman, 2014). The campaign included print ads, billboards, and online videos featuring everyday women instead of professional models.

The campaign was a massive success, resulting in a 60% increase in sales within the first two months of its launch (Harrington, 2004). Dove's "Real Beauty" campaign has been praised for its positive impact on women's self-esteem and body image and is often cited as a successful example of cause marketing.

References: Edelman (2014). Dove Campaign for Real Beauty Case Study. Retrieved from **https://www.edelman.com/work/dove-campaign-real-beauty** Harrington, S. (2004). Dove Campaign for Real Beauty. Retrieved from **https://web.archive.org/web/20070929091332/http://www.prweekus.com/Dove-Campaign-for-Real-Beauty/article/53298/**

9.1 Different Types Of Ads

In the world of advertising, there are numerous ad formats and channels to choose from, each with its unique strengths and weaknesses. Selecting the right type of ad for your campaign is crucial to maximize its impact and effectiveness. In this section, we'll explore various types of ads and how they can be utilized to reach your target audience and communicate your message effectively.

Print Ads

Print ads have been a staple of advertising for centuries, appearing in newspapers, magazines, and other print materials. Despite the rise of digital media, print ads can still be an effective way to reach specific demographics and create a lasting impression. Print ads allow for a high level of creativity in design and layout and are particularly suitable for showcasing products with strong visual appeal.

Television Ads

Television ads offer the unique advantage of combining audio and visual elements to create a memorable and engaging advertisement. With the potential for a large audience reach, television ads can be highly effective for building brand awareness and creating emotional connections with viewers. However, they can also be costly to produce and air, making them better suited for larger companies with more extensive marketing budgets.

Radio Ads

Radio ads rely on the power of sound to communicate your

message, making them ideal for reaching audiences while they're commuting, working, or relaxing at home. With lower production costs compared to television ads, radio ads can be an affordable option for businesses with limited budgets. However, the lack of visuals may make it more challenging to create an emotional connection with your audience.

Outdoor Ads

Outdoor ads, such as billboards, posters, and transit ads, are designed to capture the attention of passers-by in public spaces. They can be an effective way to build brand awareness and reach a broad audience but may have limited targeting capabilities. Outdoor ads should be visually impactful and convey your message quickly and clearly, as viewers often have limited time to process the information.

Online Display Ads

Online display ads are a popular digital advertising format, appearing on websites, apps, and social media platforms. These ads can be highly targeted, allowing you to reach specific demographics and interests. Display ads can take various forms, such as banners, video ads, and native ads, offering flexibility in design and messaging.

Social Media Ads

Social media platforms, such as Facebook, Instagram, and Twitter, offer powerful advertising opportunities to reach and engage your target audience. Social media ads can be highly targeted and provide valuable analytics to track their performance. Additionally, social media ads can encourage interaction and sharing, increasing your ad's reach and potential impact.

Search Engine Ads

Search engine ads, such as Google Ads, are a form of pay-per-click (PPC) advertising that appears alongside search engine results. These ads can be highly effective in reaching potential customers actively searching for products or services like yours. By targeting specific keywords and tailoring your ad copy to address the user's search intent, you can drive highly relevant traffic to your website.

Content Marketing Ads

Content marketing ads, such as sponsored blog posts, articles, or videos, provide valuable information or entertainment to your target audience while subtly promoting your product or service. These ads can help to establish your brand as an authority in your industry, build trust with your audience, and generate leads through valuable and engaging content.

Influencer Marketing Ads

Influencer marketing ads involve partnering with social media influencers or industry experts to promote your product or service to their followers. These ads can be highly effective in leveraging the trust and credibility that influencers have built with their audience, driving engagement and conversions.

The type of ad you choose for your campaign will depend on your objectives, target audience, and budget. By understanding the various types of ads available and their unique strengths

Case Study: Old Spice's "The Man Your Man Could Smell Like" Campaign

Old Spice's "The Man Your Man Could Smell Like" campaign, launched in 2010, is an excellent example of how humor and creativity can drive a successful marketing campaign (Effie Awards, 2011). The campaign featured a series of TV commercials and online videos starring actor Isaiah Mustafa as the charming and charismatic "Old Spice Man."

The campaign quickly went viral, garnering millions of views on YouTube and generating significant buzz on social media. As a result, Old Spice's sales increased by 107% within the first month of the campaign, and the brand successfully repositioned itself as relevant and appealing to a younger audience (Effie Awards, 2011).

*References: Effie Awards (2011). Old Spice Responses. Retrieved from **https://www.effie.org/case_database/case/NA_2011_6646***

9.2 Ad Strategies

Advertising plays a vital role in the world of sales, as it allows you to reach a wide audience and communicate the unique benefits of your product or service. To create effective ad strategies, it's essential to understand the psychology behind successful advertising and how to apply these principles to your campaigns. In this section, we'll explore a range of ad strategies that leverage the principles of psychology to capture attention, evoke emotions, and ultimately, drive sales.

The Attention-Grabbing Headline

The headline is the first element of your ad that your audience will see, and it plays a crucial role in capturing their attention. To create an attention-grabbing headline, consider using strong, action-oriented language that addresses the needs and desires of your target audience. You can also use curiosity, surprise, or humor to pique their interest and entice them to read further.

The Power of Visuals

Visuals are an essential component of effective advertising, as they help to convey your message quickly and powerfully. Use compelling images or videos that evoke emotions, showcase your product in action, or demonstrate its benefits. High-quality visuals can enhance the credibility of your ad, create an emotional connection with your audience, and improve recall.

The Emotional Appeal

As we've explored in earlier in this chapter, emotions are a powerful driver of decision-making. To create an effective ad strategy, tap into the emotions that resonate with your target audience. Consider the fears, desires, and aspirations that motivate them, and use storytelling techniques to evoke these emotions in your ad.

The Unique Selling Proposition (USP)

Your USP is the distinctive feature or benefit that sets your product or service apart from the competition. To create an impactful ad, focus on your USP and communicate it clearly and succinctly. By highlighting the unique value you offer, you can differentiate yourself in a crowded marketplace and give your audience a compelling reason to choose your product.

The Call-to-Action (CTA)

An effective ad strategy requires a clear and persuasive call-to-action that encourages your audience to take the next step in the buying process. Use action-oriented language that emphasizes the benefits your audience will receive and creates a sense of urgency. Consider using psychological principles such as scarcity and social proof to further strengthen your CTA and motivate your audience to act.

The Power of Repetition

Repetition is a powerful psychological tool that can enhance the memorability and impact of your ad. By repeating your key message or using a memorable tagline, you can reinforce your brand identity and ensure that your audience remembers your product when they're ready to make a purchase.

The Testimonial

Social proof is a potent psychological principle that can help to build trust and credibility in your ad. Include testimonials from satisfied customers or endorsements from experts in your industry to demonstrate the value of your product and reassure potential customers that they're making the right choice.

The Multi-Channel Approach

To maximize the reach and impact of your ad strategy, consider using a multi-channel approach that combines traditional and digital advertising platforms. By leveraging the strengths of various channels, such as print, television, social media, and content marketing, you can create a cohesive and powerful ad campaign that resonates with your target audience.

In summary, effective ad strategies rely on a deep understanding of the psychology behind successful advertising. By incorporating attention-grabbing headlines, powerful visuals, emotional appeals, and clear calls-to-action, you can create impactful ads that drive sales and contribute to the success of your overall marketing campaign.

> **Case Study: Coca-Cola's "Share a Coke" Campaign**
>
> *Coca-Cola's "Share a Coke" campaign, launched in 2011, is a prime example of personalization in marketing (Moye, 2014). The campaign involved replacing the iconic Coca-Cola logo on bottles and cans with popular first names, encouraging consumers to share a Coke with a friend or loved one.*
>
> *The "Share a Coke" campaign resonated strongly with consumers, resulting in a 2.5% increase in sales in the United States and reversing a decade-long decline in Coca-Cola consumption (Huddleston, 2014). The campaign's success can be attributed to its ability to create an emotional connection with consumers and leverage the power of social media to drive engagement.*
>
> *References: Moye, J. (2014). Share a Coke: How the Groundbreaking Campaign Got Its Start 'Down Under'.*

> *Retrieved from https://www.coca-colacompany.com/stories/share-a-coke-how-the-groundbreaking-campaign-got-its-start-down-under* Huddleston Jr., T. (2014). *How Coca-Cola's 'Share a Coke' Campaign Helped It To Reverse A 10-Year Decline In Sales. Retrieved from https://www.businessinsider.com/how-coca-colas-share-a-coke-campaign-helped-it-to-reverse-a-10-year-decline-in-sales-2014-10*

By examining these case studies, we can see how effective marketing campaigns can leverage various psychological principles, such as challenging societal norms, using humor and creativity, and personalizing the customer experience, to create a powerful impact and drive sales.

10

Chapter 10: Conclusion

As we reach the conclusion of "The Psychology of Selling: Mastering the Art of Influence," let us take a moment to revisit and reflect upon the key concepts and strategies that have been covered throughout this book. Our journey has spanned a wide range of topics, all aimed at providing sales professionals with a deep understanding of the psychological principles that underpin successful selling and the practical tools needed to excel in the modern sales environment.

We began by delving into the human mind and the importance of understanding your customer. This foundational knowledge allows sales professionals to better empathize with their prospects, anticipate their needs, and tailor their sales approach accordingly.

We then explored the concept of cognitive biases, which are mental shortcuts that can both help and hinder decision-making. By being aware of these biases, sales professionals can use them to their advantage while avoiding the pitfalls they may create.

Emotional intelligence was the next topic we tackled, emphasizing the importance of connecting with prospects on an emotional level to build trust and rapport. This connection is critical to influencing the decision-making process and closing deals.

First impressions were also highlighted as crucial in the sales process. We discussed the importance of making a strong and positive initial impression, as it can significantly influence how prospects perceive and interact with you throughout the sales journey.

Active listening emerged as a key skill for sales professionals, allowing them to truly understand their prospects' needs and concerns. By honing this skill, sales professionals can create stronger connections and foster more productive sales conversations.

The art of subtle influence was explored through mirroring and matching techniques, which help to create rapport and facilitate smoother communication with prospects.

We then examined the six principles of persuasion, as outlined by Dr. Robert Cialdini, which provide a valuable framework for understanding how to effectively influence others in the sales context.

Storytelling emerged as a powerful tool for captivating and engaging audiences, helping sales professionals to convey their message in a compelling and memorable way.

Framing was introduced as the art of contextualizing your message, demonstrating how sales professionals can shape the way their prospects perceive and evaluate information.

The book then delved into the important aspects of identifying and classifying objections, as well as dealing with resistance, which are both essential to overcoming obstacles and ultimately turning a 'no' into a 'yes.'

Closing the deal was covered as a critical component of the sales process, highlighting the importance of recognizing when to make the final push and how to effectively seal the deal.

Negotiation techniques for sales success were discussed, offering valuable strategies for navigating complex sales situations and achieving mutually beneficial outcomes.

Building resilience emerged as a vital skill for sales professionals, who must learn to overcome rejection and failure to persevere in their pursuit of success.

Goal setting and motivation were covered as essential elements of a successful sales mindset, helping professionals to stay focused and driven in their efforts to achieve their objectives.

Continuous learning and self-improvement were emphasized as crucial for staying ahead in the ever-evolving world of sales, ensuring that sales professionals continue to grow and adapt to the changing landscape.

We also discussed the importance of digital sales and the future of selling, including the power of social media and content marketing, email marketing, and the role of artificial intelligence in sales. Each of these aspects highlighted the need for sales professionals to embrace and adapt to the rapidly changing digital landscape.

As we conclude this journey, it is our hope that the insights and strategies shared throughout this book have provided you with a deeper understanding of the psychology of selling and equipped you with the tools and techniques needed to master the art of influence. By integrating these principles and approaches into your sales process, you will be well on your way to achieving greater success and fulfilling your potential as a sales professional.

About the Author

Marketing Consulting, Business Solutions, & Web Design.
As a marketing consultant, my goal is to help businesses achieve their marketing objectives and reach their full potential. With years of experience in the industry, I have developed a deep understanding of what it takes to create successful marketing campaigns and strategies that resonate with target audiences.

I work closely with my clients to understand their unique challenges, opportunities, and goals, and then develop tailored solutions that meet their specific needs. Whether you're looking to increase brand awareness, drive website traffic, generate leads, or boost sales, I have the expertise and know-how to help you get there.

My approach is collaborative, transparent, and results-driven. I believe in building long-term relationships with my clients based on trust, communication, and mutual respect. I am committed to delivering high-quality work that exceeds expectations and helps my clients achieve their business objectives.

If you're looking for a marketing consultant who can provide you with the strategic guidance, insights, and support you need to succeed in today's competitive marketplace, look no further. I would be honored to partner with you and help you achieve your marketing goals.

"Success usually comes to those who are too busy to be looking for it." – Henry David Thoreau

REQUEST A FREE CONSULTATION FOR MARKETING OR ADVERTISING SERVICES @ WWW.JOSHUALEEBRYANT.COM

You can connect with me on:
- https://www.joshualeebryant.com

Printed in Great Britain
by Amazon